1 MONTH OF
FREE
READING

at

www.ForgottenBooks.com

By purchasing this book you are eligible for one month membership to ForgottenBooks.com, giving you unlimited access to our entire collection of over 1,000,000 titles via our web site and mobile apps.

To claim your free month visit:

www.forgottenbooks.com/free529456

ISBN 978-0-484-42646-6
PIBN 10529456

AN ACT

TO

ESTABLISH A SYSTEM

OF

COMMON SCHOOLS,

IN THE

STATE OF CALIFORNIA;

AND

OTHER ACTS

PROVIDING FOR THE REVENUE OF THE SAME,

WITH

EXPLANATORY FORMS.

————◇————

BY JOHN G. MARVIN, LL. B.,

SUPERINTENDENT OF PUBLIC INSTRUCTION.

————◇————

SACRAMENTO:

PRINTED AT THE DEMOCRATIC STATE JOURNAL OFFICE.

1852.

784
/

AN ACT

TO

ESTABLISH A SYSTEM

OF

COMMON SCHOOLS,

IN THE

STATE OF CALIFORNIA;

AND

OTHER ACTS

PROVIDING FOR THE REVENUE OF THE SAME,

WITH

EXPLANATORY FORMS.

———— •• ————

BY JOHN G. MARVIN, LL. B.,

SUPERINTENDENT OF PUBLIC INSTRUCTION.

——————

SACRAMENTO:

PRINTED AT THE DEMOCRATIC STATE JOURNAL OFFICE.

1852.

PREFACE.

THE laws of the past session of the Legislature contained in this pamplet, are the first effective efforts that have been made on the part of the State, for the establishment and support of Free Common Schools. They are based upon the following Article of the Constitution :

ARTICLE IX.

EDUCATION.

SEC. 1. " The Legislature shall provide for the election, by the people, of a Superintendent of Public Instruction, who shall hold his office for three years, and whose duties shall be prescribed by law, and who shall receive such compensation as the Legislature may direct.

SEC. 2. The Legislature shall encourage, by all suitable means, the promotion of intellectual, scientific, moral, and agricultural improvement. The proceeds of all lands that may be granted by the United States to this State for the support of Schools, which may be sold or disposed of, and the 500,000 acres of land granted to the new States under an Act of Congress distributing the proceeds of the Public Lands among the several States of the Union, approved A. D. 1841 ; and all estates of deceased persons, who may have died without leaving a will, or heir, and also such per cent. as may be granted by Congress on the sale of lands in this State, shall be and remain a perpetual fund, the interest of which, together with all the rents of the unsold lands, and such other means as the Legislature may provide, shall be inviolably appropriated to the use of Common Schools throughout the State.

SEC. 3. The Legislature shall provide for a system of Common Schools, by which a School shall be kept up and supported in each district, at least three months in every year ; and any school district neglecting to keep up and support such a School, may be deprived of its proportion of the interest of the public fund during such neglect.

SEC. 4. The Legislature shall take measures for the protection, improvement, or other disposition of such lands as have been, or may be hereafter reserved or granted by the United States; or any person or persons, to this State for the use of a University ; and the funds acruing from the rents or sale of such lands, or from any other source for the purpose aforesaid, shall be and remain a permanent fund, the interest of which shall be applied to the support of said University, with such branches as the public convenience may demand, for the promotion of literature, the arts and sciences, as may be authorized by the terms of such grant. And it shall be the duty of the Legislature, as soon as may be, to provide effectual means for the improvement and permanent security of the funds of said University."

By section 3rd of the above Article, and section 4th, page 7, of the School law, it will be seen that the inhabitants of each School district, are required to support a School for three months during the year, to entitle them to their distributive portion of the revenue of the School fund.

It is to be hoped that all of the requirements of the School law will be complied with, since upon them, depend the value and usefulness of our Common Schools.

Under the existing statutory provisions, it is estimated that not less than $80,000 will accrue during the present year for distribution, among those districts which comply with the law.

Separate Blanks will be prepared and furnished the County Superintendents for distribution, with all convenient despatch.

JOHN G. MARVIN,

Vallejo, May 15, 1852.   Sup. Pub. Instruction.

CORRECTION.—In Forms Nos. X and XI, pages 19 and 20, insert four instead of five years.

AN ACT

ESTABLISH A SYSTEM OF COMMON SCHOOLS.

The People of the State of California represented in Senate and Assembly, do enact as follows :

ARTICLE I.

OFFICERS.

Sec. 1. The Governor, the Superintendent of Public Instruction, and the Surveyor General of the State, shall constitute, and are hereby constituted a Board of Education. The Governor shall be the President, and the Superintendent of Public Instruction shall be the Secretary of the said Board.

Sec. 2. The County Assessor of each and every county in this State, shall be, and he is hereby constituted the Superintendent of Common Schools within and for his county. (*a*)

Sec. 3. In each of the towns, cities and villages in this State, except as otherwise provided by this act, there shall be three Com-

---

(*a*) N. B. Section 2 was in the engrossed bill that passed, but was accidentally omitted in the enrolled bill.

missioners of Common Schools, who shall be annually elected at the general election, and in the same manner, as Justices of the Peace.

SEC. 4.   The three Commissioners of Common Schools, mentioned in the last preceding section, alone, or any two of them, in conjunction with the County Superintendent of Common Schools, or a Justice of the Peace of the town, city or village, shall constitute a Board of Commissioners of Common Schools for such town, city or village, as the case may be.

SEC. 5.   A Constable in each town, city and village, duly elected and qualified as such, to be selected and designated by the Board of Commissioners of Common Schools for such town, city or village, shall be the Common School Marshal therein, to take the census of the children residing within his precinct.

ARTICLE II.

SCHOOL YEAR.

SEC. 1.   The Common School year shall commence on the first day of November, and end on the last day of October.

ARTICLE III.

DUTIES AND POWERS OF OFFICERS.

SEC. 1.   The Marshals designated and selected by the Boards of Commissioners under the provisions of this Act, for the respective towns, cities and villages, shall in the month of October, annually, take a specific census of all the children within their respective precincts, between the ages of four and eighteen years, specifying the names of the children, of the parents or guardians of such children, and the town, city, village and School District, within which they reside, and make full report thereof, in writing, under oath, to the County Superintendent of Common Schools, and deliver a true copy thereof to the Boards of Commissioners in and for their respective towns, cities or villages, by the tenth day of November next thereafter.

SEC. 2. The Boards of Commissioners of Common Schools of the several towns, cities and villages, shall have power, and it shall be their duty, within their respective jurisdictions :

1. To select and designate, by writing, under their hands, one of the Constables within their respective jurisdictions, to be the Common School Marshal to take the census of the children.

2. To constitute and define, and from time to time to alter the boundaries of Common School Districts, and fix the location of School houses, in accordance with the expressed wishes of a majority of the qualified electors within such boundaries ; but in case a majority of such voters shall not agree therein, then, and in that case, the said Board of Commissioners shall, in their discretion, constitute such Common School Districts, define the boundaries thereof, and fix the locations of School Houses according to their own best judgment, and make definite reports thereof in writing, under their hands, to the County Superintendent, within ten days thereafter.

3. To audit and certify to the Superintendent of Common Schools, all accounts payable out of the State or county school fund, specifying what portion of said school fund is chargeable with the same.

4. To superintend the erection and repairs of all School Houses in the several Common School Districts, or appoint a Building Committee in such districts respectively, for that purpose, who shall be subject to the instructions and supervision of such Board of Commissioners of Common Schools ; to distribute the blank forms, laws and instructions received by them from the county superintendent to the common school marshals and teachers, who shall be by the provisions of this Act entitled to receive the same.

5. To hold meetings so often as they shall deem necessary for the examination of persons preposing to become Common School

Teachers, under the provisions of this Act; and to grant certificates of approbation and recommendation to such as they shall find, on a rigid and thorough examination and investigation, to be persons of good moral character, of sufficient learning and ability for teaching, having a special regard to their ability to impart knowledge—and to no others—and to revoke any such certificate at pleasure. All such certificates shall remain in force during one year from and after their respective dates, unless sooner revoked, and no longer; and any certificate, otherwise granted, shall be void.

6. To employ and fix the salaries and terms of service of the Common School Teachers.

7. To suspend or expel from any such Common School, with the advice of the Teacher, any pupil who will not submit to the reasonable and ordinary rules of order and discipline therein.

8. To apportion the Common Schools among the members of the Board, in such manner that at least one of the said Commissioners shall visit and ascertain the character, progress and prospects of each school, and report the same to the full Board, once a quarter.

9. To carry out and execute their powers and duties, as conferred and imposed by this Act, in accordance with the instructions of the State Board of Education, and in manner and in form as shall be prescribed by the Superintendent of Public Instruction.

10. To make and keep a record of all their official acts and decisions, and a strict and particular account of all bills audited and certified to the county superintendent; said record and account, together with the vouchers relating thereto, shall be subject, at all times, to the inspection and examination of the State Superintendent of Public Instruction, or the County Superintendent of Common Schools.

11. To report to the County Superintendent of Common Schools of their respective counties, on or before the 15th day of November, annually, the amount of all expenditures on account of schools in their respective precincts, during the previous school year, ending on the last day of October; and the manner in which the same shall have been expended, specifying what portion and amount thereof has been expended for the services of legally qualified Teachers; the amounts which, during that time, shall have been raised in the several Common School Districts, by subscription or otherwise, and allowed to such qualified Teachers, as salary or compensation; the names of the Teachers employed; the time of service, and the salaries paid to each; the number of pupils . taught, and the average attendance and progress of the pupils in each school organized and taught under the provisions of this Act, and such other statistics as shall be required by the Superintendent of Public Instruction.

12. And, at the close of their official term, to deliver over their Book of Records, and all papers, books, blanks, and documents in their hands, as such Commissioners, to their successors in office, and take their receipt for the same, which receipt shall be filed with the County Superintendent.

SEC. 3. The County Superintendent of Common Schools in and for each County, shall have power, in accordance with the principles and provisions of this Act, and the instructions of the State Board of Education, and of the Superintendent of Public Instruction :

1. To exercise a general supervision over the interests of Common Schools in his County, and to give to the Commissioners of Common Schools, the Common School Marshals, and Common School Teachers, such aid and counsel as may be important to the prosperity of the Schools.

2. To distribute promptly to the Commissioners of Common Schools, such blank Reports, Forms, Laws and instructions as shall

be deposited in his office by the Superintendent of Public Instruction—for the use of the Commissioners, Teachers and Marshals, and any other officers within the several counties entitled to the same.

3. To draw his warrants on the County Treasurer in favor of, and deliver the same to, the persons holding accounts audited and certified by the Boards of Commissioners of Common Schools, under the provisions of this Act; *Provided,* that no such warrant shall be drawn until full and correct returns shall have been made to him by said Board of Commissioners.

4. To appoint, upon the passage of this Act, three qualified electors of each town, city and village, within his county (unless otherwise provided by law,) to be Commissioners of Common Schools therein, until the next general election, who shall exercise all the powers, and perform all the duties hereinbefore conferred and imposed upon Commissioners of Common Schools, until superseded by an election, and from time to time to fill, by such appointment, any vacancy which shall occur in any Board of Commisioners of Common Schools, until a new election.

5. To keep on file in his office the Reports of the Common School Marshals and of the Commissioners of Common Schools, received by him, and to record the material parts thereof, together with all his official acts as such County Superintendent of Common Schools, in a book to be provided for that purpose, and at the close of his official term, to deliver over to his successor, such records, and all documents, books and papers belonging to his department, and take his receipt for the same, which shall be filed in the office of the County Treasurer.

6. To make full report in writing, annually, in the month of November, for the school year, ending on the last day of October next previous thereto, to the Superintendent of Public Instruction, and deliver a copy thereof to the County Treasurer of his Coun-

ty, in such form and manner as shall be prescribed by the said Superintendent of Public Instruction.

SEC. 4. The Common School moneys in the County Treasuries, shall be apportioned among the several towns, cities, and villages, in proportion to the number of children residing therein, between the ages of five and eighteen years, as shown by the last previous reports of the Common School Marshals, and other officers charged therewith; and no School District shall be entitled to any portion of the Common School moneys, in which there shall not have been taught, by a legally qualified Teacher, a Common School for three months, within the year ending on the last day of October, and one half of the compensation of said Teacher paid by the inhabitants of said district.

SEC. 5. It shall be the duty of the County Treasurer of each and every county:

1. To receive and hold, as a special deposit, all Common School moneys, whether received by him from the State Treasury or raised by the County, for the benefit of Common Schools, and to keep a separate account thereof, and of their disbursements.

2. On receiving any Common School moneys for distribution, to notify the County Superintendent of Common Schools, of the amount thereof, and the shares to which the several towns, cities, villages, and School Districts are entitled, under the provisions of this Act.

3. To pay over, on the warrant of the County Superintendent, duly endorsed by one or more of the commissioners aforesaid, and by the teacher or other persons to whom due, the several amounts of Common School moneys to which each district shall be lawfully entitled.

4. And on or before the fifteenth day of November, annually, to make full report of the Common School moneys received into the County Treasury, within the School year ending on the last

day of October next previous thereto, with a particular statement of the disbursement of the said School moneys, and of any amount of such School moneys which may remain in his hands for distribution, at the close of such School year, to the State Superintendent of Public Instruction.

SEC. 6. It shall be the duty of the State Treasurer to receive, and hold, as a special deposit, all Common School moneys paid into the Treasury, and to pay them over only by order of the State Board of Education upon the warrant of the Superintendent of Public Instruction, under the Common Seal of the said Board of Education, to the county Treasurers; and such warrants, duly endorsed by the County Treasurers, shall be the only valid vouchers in the hands of the State Treasurer for the disbursement of the said common school moneys.

SEC .7. The school moneys distributed to the various Counties of this State from the State School Fund, shall not be issued for any other purpose than the payment of the salaries of qualified Teachers under this Act; and no portion of said fund shall either directly or indirectly, be paid for the erection of school houses, the use of school rooms, furniture or any other contingent expenses of common schools.

SEC. 8. Not less than fifty per cent. of the school fund raised by county tax and paid into the county treasury, shall be paid for any other purpose than the payment of qualified teachers; and the residue of the moneys distributed to the several districts.— From the County school fund may be appropriated, for the purchase of a district school library, to build a district school house, or such other contingent expenses of the school, as the School Commissioners of each district shall determine.

ARTICLE IV.

SUPERINTENDENT OF PUBLIC INSTRUCTION.

SEC. 1. It shall be the duty of the Superintendent of Public In-struction, and he is hereby empowered, by and with the advice, and subject to the supervision of the State Board of Education.

1. To prepare and cause to be published in connection with this Act, suitable instructions and forms for the direction of the Super-intendents, Commissioners, Marshals, and Teachers of common schools; and to cause to be deposited in the office of each County Superintendent a sufficient number of copies, (in his discretion,) of this Act, and of the said instructions and forms for the supply of the common school offcers therein.

2. By lectures and by letters, publications and personal inter-views with the friends of popular education in the State, to endeav-or, to the extent of his ability, to disseminate intelligence among the people in relation to the methods and value of education, and especially in relation to common schools, and to endeavor to secure the sympathies and co-operation of the people in all Educa-tional measures which may be adopted by the Legislature.

3. To open a correspondence with Officers and Boards of Edu-cation in other States, and by means of the exchange of letters and reports with them, to make himself acquainted with the progress of educational movements and the details of public school systems in other States, to the end that the best possible system of education may be adopted for this State.

4. To exercise a general supervision over such Normal Schools, Teachers Institutes, and High Schools, as may by law be estab-lished.

5. Immediately after the State Treasurer shall have made his annual report, as hereinbefore required, to apportion to the several counties, towns, cities, villages and school districts, the amount of

school moneys in the State Treasury to which each shall be entitled under the provisions of this Act, and thereupon to make a record thereof in the book of records to be kept by the State Board of Education, and furnish to each County Treasurer and to each County Superintendent an abstract of such apportionment, specifying the amounts of common school moneys to which the several towns, cities, villages and school districts are entitled; and with such apportionment, to furnish to each County Treasurer his warrant on the State Treasurer, under the Seal of the State Board of Education, for the amount of school moneys in the State Treasury to which such County shall be legally entitled, under the apportionment above specified, and take such County Treasurer's receipt for the same.

6. To present to the Legislature at the commencement of the next session, and thereafter annually at the commencement of each session, a full report of the condition of Public Instruction in the State, the number and grade of schools in each county, the number of children in each county, between the ages of five and eighteen years; the number of such attending common schools, under the instruction of teachers qualified and employed under the provisions of this Act; the amount of common school moneys apportioned to each county; the amount thereof expended in teacher's salaries; the erection and repairs of common school houses; in the purchase of common school libraries and apparatus; the amount of moneys raised and expended in and by any county, town, city, village or school district for the support of common schools therein under the instruction of teachers holding valid certificates from the Boards of Commissioners of common schools, and duly employed and reported by such Commissioners as hereinbefore provided, together with such suggestions as he may deem it expedient to make, in relation

to the construction of school houses, the improvement and better management of common schools, the qualifications of common school teachers, the character and kinds of school books most suitable for use in common schools, the ways and means for raising funds for the support of common schools and providing suitable houses therefor, and for the promotion of the general interests of education throughout the State

7. And to superintend the printing and distribution of his annual reports in such manner as the Legislature shall from time to time direct.

ARTICLE V.
CITIES.

SEC. 1. The common council of each and every incorporated city in this State shall be, and hereby are authorized and empowered :

1st. To raise annually, by tax upon the real estate and personal property within the city, as estimated by the city assessors, whatever amount of money shall be requisite, not to exceed three cents on each $100 of valuation, for the support of a competent number of free common schools therein, and providing and furnishing suitable houses therefor.

2. To provide, by ordinance, for the collection, custody and disbursement of the moneys thus raised, by city tax, for school purposes.

3. To provide, by ordinance, for drawing from the county treasury, on the warrant of the county superintendent of common schools, the common school moneys to which such city shall be entitled, under the provisions of this Act, and for the custody and disbursement of such common school moneys, in accordance with the provisions of this Act.

4. To provide, by ordinance, for the examination of common school teachers, the regulation of common schools within the city, the census or enumeration of the children, and for making the anual and other reports to the County Superintendent of common schools.

5. To provide, by ordinance, for the election or appointment of a city board of education and Superintendent of common schools, and prescribe their powers and duties, and—

6. To ordain all such rules and regulations as they may deem expedient and necessary for the promotion of the interests, prosperity and usefulness of the common schools within the city; *Provided*, that the common council shall not make any ordinance nor do any act which shall be in conflict with the principles or provisions of the constitution of the State or of any act of the Legislature.

SEC. 2. No board of commissioners, nor marshals elected or appointed under the foregoing provisions of this Act, shall have any jurisdiction or control, within the chartered limits of any city which shall have provided for the support, regulation and management of common schools therein, under the provisions of this chapter.

ARTICLE VI.
SCHOOLS.

SEC. 1. No common school shall receive any benefits or immunities under the provisions of this Act, unless such school shall be instructed by a teacher or teachers duly examined, approved and employed by competent and lawful authority, as hereinbefore provided, nor unless such schools shall be free from all denominational and sectarian bias, control and influence whatsoever.

SEC. 2. The boards of commissioners may cause the common schools, within their respective jurisdictions, to be divided into primary, secondary and grammar schools, having reference to the proficiency of the pupils, and to employ competent and legally qualified teachers for the instruction of the different departments, whenever they shall deem such division into departments necessary.

SEC. 3. No school book, nor other book of a sectarian or denominational character, shall be intoduced or used in any common school instituted under the provisions of this Act.

ARTICLE VII.

COUNTIES.

SEC. 1. Each and every county in this State is hereby empowered and authorized to raise annually, by special tax, (in the same manner that other county taxes shall be levied,) upon the real estate and personal property within the county, an amount of money not exceeding three cents on each $100 of valuation, for the support of common schools therein, and for providing suitable houses and purchasing libraries and apparatus for such common schools.

SEC. 2. All moneys raised by county tax as above provided, for common school purposes, shall be paid into the county treasury as a special deposit, and shall be apportioned by the County Superintendent of common schools among the towns, cities, villages and school districts in the county, upon the basis provided by this Act for the apportionment of the State school moneys, and drawn from the county treasury, in the same manner.

ARTICLE VIII.

TEACHERS.

SEC. 1. No teacher shall be entitled to any portion of the public common school moneys hereinbefore provided for, as compensation or salary for services rendered, unless such teacher shall have been duly employed by competent authority, nor unless such teacher shall have had, during the whole time of such service, such certificate of competency and approval as is provided by this Act, in full force and effect, and bearing date within one year next before the services aforesaid shall have been rendered, nor unless such teacher shall have made report in manner and form as shall be prescribed by the Superintendent of Public Instruction.

SEC. 2. A State convention of common school teachers, commissioners of common schools, county and city Superintendents of common schools, may be holden annually at the State Capitol on the call of the Superintendent of Public Instruction, who shall preside at such convention.

SEC. 3. Such State convention may discuss and recommend improvements in teaching and the management of schools, and a series of school books for use in the common schools throughout the State, and such other topics and subjects as shall be brought before the convention by the Superintendent of Public Instruction.

ARTICLE IX.

PRINTING.

SEC. 1. Any printing called for by this Act, shall be executed in the form and manner and at the prices prescribed by law for other State printing, and shall be paid for in like manner out of the general fund, upon the bill for the same being certified to by the Board of Education.

ARTICLE X.

REPEAL.

SEC. 1. The act entitled "an Act concerning common schools and public instruction," approved May 1, 1851, is hereby repealed.

Signed May 3d, 1852.

RICHARD P. HAMMOND,
Speaker of the Assembly.

SAMUEL PURDY,
President of the Senate.

JOHN BIGLER, Governor.

FORMS.

The following forms have been drawn to assist school officers in carrying out the provisions of the preceding Act, and to secure uniformity so far as is practicable :

NO. I.

Appointment of a School Commissioner.

By authority of law, I do hereby appoint you a Commissioner of Common Schools in   , to hold your office until the next general election, and to exercise all the powers and perform all the duties conferred by law upon such an officer, by virtue of the appointment.

185 .

,

County Superintendent of Com. Schools.

NOTE —By reference to Act I, Sec. 2, of the School Act, it will be seen that the County Assessors are the County Superintendents of Common Schools, and that they have the power of appointing the School Commissioners. See page 6, rule 4.

NO. II.

Certificate of Election of a Commissioner of Common Schools.

To   OF   GREETING :

This certifies that you, the said   , were at the general election, held on the   day of   , A. D. 185 , chosen to the office of Commissioner of Common Schools of (the town or city as the case may be,) and are by virtue of said election fully authorized and empowered to discharge all the duties of said office, and to exercise all the powers thereto belonging, according to law.

NO. III.

Appointment of a Common School Marshal.

We, the undersigned, Commissioners of Common Schools for
, in the county of
, appoint ,
a duly elected and qualified Constable, Common School Marshal to take the census of the children in said
and county.

, ⎫ Commissioners
, ⎬ of
, ⎭ Com. Schools.

185 .

NOTE.—See Sec. 5, page 2, and Sec. 2, Art. V.

NO. IV.

Certificate of Qualification to keep a School.

We, the undersigned, Commissioners of Common Schools, hereby certify, that we have personally examined
and are satisfied that   is of good moral character and pos-
sesses sufficient learning and ability to teach and impart knowledge, and govern a school, we therefore grant to
this our certificate, which shall remain in force during one year
from date, unless sooner revoked.

, ⎫ Commissioners
, ⎬ of
, ⎭ Com. Schools.

185 .

NOTE.—See Rule 5, page 4, and Sec. I.

NO. V.

Form for annulling a Certificate.

Whereas the Commissioners of Common Schools, for the of , did, on the day of . , A. D. 185 , issue to a certificate of qualification as a Teacher in said · : now know ye that, upon further investigation and trial, the said has been found deficient and unqualified, (or has refused to conform to the regulations made by law;) we do therefore declare the said certificate to be annulled and void from this date, of which all persons, whose duty it is to employ teachers of common schools, are hereby requested to take notice.

, ⎫ Commissioners
, ⎬ of
, ⎭ Com. Schools.

County of   185 .

Note.—It would be proper that notice of the annulling should be given to the County Superintendent.

———

NO. VI.
Form of a Receipt of the County Superintendent of Common Schools.

Received of ,
County Superintendent of Common Schools, all documents, books and papers belonging to his office, as such Superintendent.

,
County Superintendent Com. Schools.
185 .

Note.—The law requires this receipt to be filed in the office of the County Treasurer. See page 6, Rule 5.

NO. VII.

Form of a Receipt of the Commissioners of Common Schools under Art. III, Sec. 2, Rule 12.

Received of
Commissioners of Common Schools for   .   ,
the book of records, and all papers, books, blanks and documents remaining in their hands as such Commissioners.

,⎫ Commissioners
,⎬   of
,⎭ Com. Schools.

A. D. 185 .

NO. VIII.

*Form of a Report of the Commissioners of Common Schools to the County Superintendent for the County of   ,
Town or City of   , in relation to the Boundaries and Number of School Districts.*

We, the undersigned, Commissioners of Common Schools in the county and   aforesaid, in conformity with law, do report :

That the whole number of School Districts in our
is   , and are bounded as follows : District **No. I,**
(here describe the boundaries, and location of school-houses.)

,⎫ Commissioners
,⎬   of
,⎭ Com. Schools.

185 .

Note.—This report must be made to the County Superintendent within ten days after the division into districts is agreed upon. See page 3, Rule 2.

NO. IX.

Form of County Superintendent's Warrant upon the County Treasurer.

No. ————   185 .

    The Treasurer of the County of

will pay to the order of

                dollars on account of

$————   ,

           County Superintendent Com. Schools.

Note.—See Rule 3d, pages 6 and 7.

————

NO. X.

CENSUS RETURNS.

Report of the Common School Marshal to the County Superintendent for the School-year ending October 31st, 185 .

Name of County.	Name of town, village or city.	Name or number of school district.	Names of parents or guardians.	Names of the children between the ages of five and eighteen.	No. of boys.	No. of girls.	Total amount of children.

Form of an Affidavit to be appended to the Census Returns.

County of   ,} ss.

    On this   day of   A. D.

185 , personally appeared before me the undersigned, a Justice

of the Peace for the county and   aforesaid,
a duly appointed Common School
Marshal, whose signature is hereunto subscribed, and being
sworn according to law, made oath that the facts set forth in
the above Report are just and true according to the best of his
knowledge and belief.

Justice of the Peace.

      Common School Marshal
      for

NOTE.—This Report must be made out in duplicate. See Art. III, Sec. 1.

NO. XI.

*Report of the Commissioners of Common Schools to the County
Superintendent for the County of*   ,
(Town, City or Village of   ,) *from*
    185 , *to*   185 .

Name or number of School District.	No. of children between the ages of five and eighteen.	Number of boys.	Number of girls.	Amount raised by subscription or otherwise and paid teachers.	Names of teachers employed	Grade of school.	Time of service of teachers.	Salaries paid each teacher.	No. pupils taught.	Daily average attendance.	Am't exp'd for sch'l libraries &c.	Am't expended for build'g, renting or furnishing school houses.	Total am't of all expenditures on acc't of schools.

NOTE.—When the above blank is filled up, which must be done on or before
November 15th, of each year, the following certificate should be appended. See
page 5, Rule 11.

.We, the undersigned, Commissioners of Common Schools for
the county (town or village) aforesaid, certify, on honor, that the

above is a true statement of the condition of the Common
Schools.

, ⎫ Commissioners
, ⎬ of
, ⎭ Com. Schools.

To   Esq.,
                County Superintendent
                of Common Schools.

NOTE.—The Commissioners will accompany their Report as above with such
remarks as they may think the interest of the Common School system in their
town or city may require. This will enable the County Superintendent to furnish the State Superintendent with valuable information for his Annual Report.
The report must be made on or before the 15th day of November, annually.

NO. XII.

Report of the County Treasurer to the Superintendent of Public
Instruction for the County of
from   , 185   to   185 .

Name of town, city or village.	Name or number of district.	Amount of school moneys collected under Art. I, Sec. 17, of the revenue law.	Amount of county tax collected for school purposes.	Am't pd'd teacher's salaries.	Am't p'd for erection, rents, or repairs of school houses.	Am't p'd for school libraries and apparatus.	Total am't of school moneys from all sources.	Amount of school moneys on hand.

Form of an Affidavit to be appended to the above Report.

COUNTY OF $\quad$,} ss.

On this $\qquad$ day of $\qquad$,
A. D. 185 , personally appeared before me the undersigned, a
Justice of the Peace for the county and $\qquad$ aforesaid, $\qquad$, County Treasurer for
said county, whose signature is hereunto subscribed, and being
duly sworn made oath that the facts set forth in the above report are just and true, according to the best of his knowledge
and belief.

$\qquad$,
Justice of the Peace.

$\qquad$, ESQ.,
County Treasurer.

NOTE.—See page 7, Sec. 5.

NO. XIII.

Report of the County Superintendent of Common Schools to the State Superintendent of Public Instruction for the County of 185 , from , to 185 .

Names of towns or cities.	Name or number of district.	Number from which reports have been received.	No. of children between the ages of five and eighteen.	No. of pupils attending school.	Amount raised by subscription or otherwise, and p'd teachers.	Amount expended in the erection, rents or repairs of school houses.	Amount expended for school libraries and apparatus.	Names of teachers employed.	Salaries per month paid each teacher.	Time of service of teacher.	Grade of school.	Number of boys.	Number of girls.	Daily average attendance.	Names of the Commissioners of Common Schools.	Amount of county tax assessed for school purposes.	Valuation of taxable property in the county.	Amount of school money assessed under Art. I, Sec. XVII, revenue law.	Total amount of all receipts on account of salaries.	Total amount of expenditures.

Form of an Affidavit to be appended to the preceding Report.

COUNTY OF $\left. \begin{array}{c} , \\ . \end{array} \right\}$ ss.

On this   day of   , A. D.
185 , personally appeared before me the undersigned, a Justice of the Peace for the county and   aforesaid,   , County Superintendent of
Common Schools for said county, whose signature is hereunto
subscribed, and being duly sworn made oath that the facts set
forth in the above Report are just and true according to the best
of his knowledge and belief.

,

Justice of the Peace.

,
Superintendent of Common Schools.

NOTE.—The County Superintendents are desired to fill the preceding Report,
and add thereto such accompanying observations as they may think will pro-
mote the interests of education in their counties and the State. It is desirable
to know the kind of school books used, with a view to the introduction, as soon
as practicable, of a uniform series throughout the State. Too great impor-
tance cannot be placed upon the necessity of prompt and efficient school organ-
izations under the provisions of the School Act, and regular returns made during the month of November to the Superintendent of Public Instruction. See
page 6, Rule 6.

NO. XIV.

Report of the Common School in District No. 185 in the of 185

from to Teacher.

Whole number of Children in the District between the ages of four and eighteen years

No. of Pupils.	Names of Pupils.	Age.	Females.	Males.	Orthography.	Reading.	Writing.	Vocal Music	Geography.	Arithmetic.	English Grammar	Elocution.	Natural Philosophy	History.	Rhetoric	Chemistry	Astronomy.	Geometry.	Algebra.	Latin	Greek	French.	Spanish	German	Date of Entrance.	Time of Continuance.	Grade of School.	Average daily attendance	Names of Commissioners of Common Schools.	Time when School visited, and by whom.	School Books used.
															BRANCHES TAUGHT.																

I certify on honor that the above is a true statement of the condition of the Common School in the town of County of Teacher.

NOTE.—The teacher will make the above report to the Commissioners of Common Schools, and also to the County Superintendent, which reports must be made on or before the 15th day of November of each year.

ACTS

PROVIDING FOR THE

REVENUE OF COMMON SCHOOLS.

ACTS

AN ACT

CONCERNING ESCHEATED ESTATES.

The People of the State of California, represented in Senate and Assembly, do enact as follows :

SEC. 1.   That if any person shall die, or any person who may have died, in this State, seized of any real or personal estate, without any devise thereof, and leaving no heirs or representatives capable of inheriting the same, or the devisees thereof be incapable of holding the same, and in all cases where there is no owner of such real estate, capable of holding the same, such estate shall escheat to and be vested in this State.

SEC. 2.   That whenever the Attorney-General, or District Attorney, shall be informed, or have reason to believe, that any real estate in his district hath escheated to the State. by reason that any person hath died seized thereof, without devising the same, and leaving no heirs capable of inheriting the same, or by reason of the incapacity of the devisees to hold the same, and such estate shall not have been sold, according to law, within two years after the death of the person last seized, or when he shall be informed or has cause to believe that any such estate within his district hath otherwise escheated to the State, it shall be his duty to file an information, in behalf of the State, in the District Court of the Judicial District, or of any adjoining judicial district, in which such estate is situated, setting forth a description of the estate, the name of the person last lawfully seized, the name of the *terre-tenant* and persons claiming such estate, if known, and the facts and circumstances in consequence of which such estate is claimed to have escheated, and alleging that by reason thereof the State of California hath right by law to such estate : whereupon such Court shall award and issue a summons against such person or persons, bodies politic or corporate, as shall be alleged in such information to hold, possess or claim such estate, requiring them to appear and show cause why such estate should not be vested in the State, on the first day of the next regular term of said Court ; which summons shall be served at least fifteen days before the return day thereof ; and the Court, moreover, shall make an order setting forth briefly the contents of such information, and requiring all persons interested in the estate to appear and show cause, if any they have, on the first day of the next term of the said Court, why the same should not vest in the State ; which order shall be published in a newspaper, published in said district, if one be published therein, and in case no newspaper should be published in said district, the same to be published by direction of the Judge in some other newspaper in this State.

Sec. 3. All persons, bodies politic and corporate, named in such information as *terre-tenant*, or claimant to the estate, may appear and plead to such proceeding, and may traverse or deny the facts stated in the information, the title of the State to lands and tenements therein mentioned, at any time on or before the third day of the return day of the summons ; and any other person claiming an interest in such estate may appear and be made a defendant, and plead as aforesaid, by motion for that purpose in open court, within the time allowed for pleading as aforesaid ; and if any person shall appear and plead as aforesaid, or shall refuse to plead within the time, then judgment shall be rendered that the State be seized of the lands and tenements in such information claimed. But if any person shall appear and deny the title set up by the State, or traverse any material fact set forth in the information, or issue or issues, shall be made up and tried as other issues of fact, and a survey may be ordered and entered as in other actions when the title or boundary is drawn in question ; and if after the issues are tried, it shall appear from the facts, found or admitted, that the State hath good title to the land and tenements in the information mentioned, or any part thereof, judgment shall be rendered that the State be seized thereof, and recover costs of suit against the defendants.

SEC. 4. Any party who shall have appeared to any proceedings, as aforesaid, and the Attorney-General or District Attorney in behalf of the State, shall respectively have the same right to prosecute an appeal or writ of error upon any judgment, as aforesaid, as parties in other cases.

SEC. 5. The Comptroller of State shall keep just and true accounts of all moneys paid into the treasury, all lands vested in the State, as aforesaid ; and if any person shall appear within ten years after the death of the intestate, and claim any moneys paid into the treasury, as aforesaid, as heir or legal representative, such person may file a petition to the District Court in which the Seat of Government may be staying, stating the nature of his claim, and praying such money may be paid him ; a copy of such petition shall be served on the Attorney-General at least twenty days before the hearing of said petition, who shall put in answer to the same, and the Court thereupon shall examine said claim. and the allegations and proofs; and if the Court shall find that such person is entitled to any money paid into the State treasury, he shall by an order, direct the Comptroller to issue his warrant on the treasury for the payment of the same, but without interest or cost to the State; a copy of which order, under the seal of the Court, shall be a sufficient voucher for issuing such warrant; and if any person shall appear and claim land vested in the State, as aforesaid, within five years after the judgment was rendered, it shall be lawful for such person (other than such as was served with a summons or appeared to the proceeding, their heirs or assigns,) to file in the said District Court, in which the lands claimed lie, a petition setting forth the nature of his claim, and praying that the said lands may be relinquished to him; a copy of which petition shall be served on the Attorney-General, who shall put in an answer, and the Court thereupon shall examine said claim, allegations and proofs, and if it shall appear that such person is entitled to such land claimed, the Court shall decree accordingly, which shall be effectual for divesting the interest of the State in or to the lands; but no costs shall be charged to the State; and all persons who shall fail to appear and file their petition, within the time limited as aforesaid, shall be forever barred; saving, however, infants, married women, and persons of unsound mind, or persons beyond the limits of the United States, the right to appear and file their petition, as aforesaid, at any time within five years after their respective disabilities are removed : *Provided, however*, that the Legislature may cause such lands to be sold at any time after seizure, in such manner as may be provided by law; in which case the claimants shall be entitled to the proceeds, in lieu of such lands, upon obtaining a decree or order as aforesaid.

APPROVED May 4, 1852.

AN ACT

To provide for the Disposal of the Five Hundred Thousand Acres of Land Granted to this State by Act of Congress.

That the people of the State of California may avail themselves of the benefits of the eighth section of the act of Congress, approved 4th of April, 1841, chapter 16, entitled an act to appropriate the proceeds of the sales of the Public Lands and to grant Pre-emption Rights, the following provisions are hereby enacted.

The people of the State of California, represented in Senate and assembly, do enact as follows :

SEC. 1. The Governor of this State is hereby authorized to issue land warrants for not less than one hundred and sixty, and not more than three hundred and twenty acres in one warrant to the amount of five hundred thousand acres, which warrants, when so signed and issued by the Governor, shall be countersigned by the Comptroller, and by him deposited in the office of the Treasurer of State for sale, charging the same to account of the Treasurer.

SEC. 2. The Treasurer of State is hereby authorized, on application to him therefor, to sell said land warrants for two dollars per acre, in the lawful currency of the United States, in State scrip, or Comptroller's warrants, drawn upon the general fund, or bonds of the civil debt of the State, now due, the interest, if any thereon, to be included in the aggregate of such payment, and the said Treasurer is required to convert all lawful moneys of the United States, and all State three per cent. bonds, or Comptroller's warrants so received by him into bonds, of the civil funded debt of the State, bearing seven per cent. interest per annum, and to keep such bonds as a special deposit in his custody, marked "School Fund," to the credit of said School Fund. All interest falling due on said bonds so set apart to the credit of the School Fund, shall be semi-annually placed to the credit of said School Fund. All State three per cent. bonds or Comptroller's warrants so converted by him into seven per cent. bonds, as above provided, shall be cancelled and destroyed in the manner now provided by law.

SEC. 3. The parties purchasing such warrants and their assigns, are hereby authorized, in behalf of this State, to locate the same upon any vacant and unappropriated lands belonging to the United States, within the State of California, subject to such location, but no such location shall be made, unless it be made in conformity to the law of Congress, which law provides that not less than three hundred and twenty acres shall be located in a body.

SEC. 4. Lands thus located shall be run off by a line, north and south and east and west, and shall be sufficiently designated by lines and distances, corners or posts, as the case may be, and an entry made thereof in the office of the Clerk of the County Court of the county in which such lands shall be located.

SEC. 5. The location made of the lands belonging to the United States, as aforesaid, shall secure to the purchaser the right of possession to the land embraced within said survey until such time as the Government survey shall have been made, after which, said lines shall be made to conform to the lines of sections, quarter sections, and fractional sections of said government survey ; and in the event that two or more persons shall have made the location on the same section, quarter section, or fractional section, then, and in that event, the person whose location embraces the largest portion of said section, quarter section, or fractional section shall be first entitled to said location of the same.

Sec. 6. If in the survey to be hereafter made by the General Government, it should so happen that the improvement made by any person purchasing and locating lands under this act, shall not compose the larger part of the first survey, then, and in that case, the party may, if they prefer it, retain that portion which has upon it their buildings and improvements, although it may be the smaller portion of said section, quarter section, or fractional section. Provided nothing herein contained shall authorize such location upon any lands heretofore granted by this State, or by the General Government, or on lands at the time of such survey and location, actually occupied and improved by actual settlers, unless such location be made by the owner of such improvement, not to exceed six hundred and forty acres by any one person. Provided, also, that nothing herein contained shall prejudice the ownership or possession of any lands at the time of said survey and location, held or claimed under grants from the Mexican or Spanish governments, and provided moreover, that at the time of making such location the first settler, or owner of any improvement situated on the tract proposed to be located, shall in all cases have the preference.

Sec. 7. In the event that any location of lands be made under and by the provisions of this Act, upon lands supposed to belong to the United States, which should prove to be land not the property of the United States, then and in that case the party owning such land warrant or warrants may float the same upon any other public lands in the State of California, provided the float and the reasons therefor be made a matter of record at the time, in the office where the original location was recorded.

SEC. 8.   The Comptroller shall keep an accurate account of the quantity of land thus disposed of, in accordance with the provisions of the foregoing sections, and the amounts received by the Treasurer, charging the several sums thus received to the Treasurer, which sum or sums shall be set aside for a general fund to meet the liabilities of the State.

SEC. 9.   The interest upon the sum thus realized by the sale of the five hundred thousand acres of land granted to this State, by act of Congress, shall be and the same is hereby set apart as a permanent fund for the support of schools, in accordance with the Constitution of the State of California.

SEC. 10.   Lands located under the provisions of this Act, shall be surveyed by the County Surveyor, in each county where the location is made, who shall give a certificate setting forth the bounds and the number of acres contained in such survey, and shall receive for his services such fees as are now or may hereafter be provided by law.

SEC. 11.   The Clerk of the County Court shall make a record of all certificates of land located under the provisions of this Act which may have been run off by the proper officer, and shall be entitled to receive from the owner of such location three dollars for such services.

SEC. 12.   The County Surveyors of the respective counties of this State, at the end of every three months from the taking effect of this Act, shall make out and forward to the office of the Surveyor-General of the State, without fee for the same, a duplicate copy of each plot or survey and certificate of the location of any land warrant made under the provisions of this Act, in their respective counties, and for failure so to do shall be liable to a fine of not less than five hundred or more than five thousand dollars, recoverable before any court of competent jurisdiction on the complaint of any person or persons in interest.

SEC. 13. The interest to be credited to the school fund on all moneys received into the State Treasury under the provisions of this Act, shall be calculated at the rate of seven per centum per annum, until the Legislature shall otherwise direct.

SEC. 14. So soon as the lands which may be located under and by virtue of the provisions of this Act, shall have been surveyed by the United States, and such locations are made to conform thereto, the Governor of this State shall cause patents to be issued in such manner and form as the Legislature may hereafter direct.

SEC. 15. No person shall be permitted to purchase under this Act, warrants for more than six hundred and forty acres, and shall before purchasing one of said warrants, deposit with the Comptroller an affidavit setting forth that he wants said lands for the purpose of making a permanent settlement thereon.

SEC. 16. It shall not be lawful to locate any of said warrants upon the land within the limits of any town now surveyed or laid off.

SEC. 17. This Act to take effect and be in force from and after the first day of June, eighteen hundred and fifty-two.

APPROVED May 3, 1852.

RICHARD P. HAMMOND,
Speaker of the Assembly.

SAMUEL PURDY,
President of the Senate.

JOHN BIGLER, Governor.

AN ACT

To provide for Levying, Assessing and Collecting Public Revenue.

SEC. 2.   The amount of Property Tax levied by this Act, shall be thirty cents on each one hundred dollars' worth of all real and personal property in this State, for State purposes, except as hereinafter provided ; and an additional amount, not exceeding fifty cents on each one hundred dollars' worth thereof, for County purposes.

SEC. 17.   Between the first Monday of March and July of each year, the County Assessor shall ascertain, by dilligent inquiry and examination through all the inhabited portions of his County, the names of all taxable inhabitants, and the full amount of all the real and personal property within the County which is not exempt from taxation by this Act; and all the real and personal property in this State not so exempt, shall be liable for the payment of not more than the amount specified in the second section of this Act ; and the whole amount thereof required for State purposes, as provided in the second section of this Act, is hereby appropriated, as follows : five cents of the thirty cents imposed on each one hundred dollars, is exacted for the sole purpose and shall be retained by the Treasurer of the State and paid out only as the laws for the benefit of the Common Schools of this State shall direct ; fifteen cents of the said thirty cents imposed for the payment of the Interest Tax, as funded in the Act to fund the debt of the State ; and the remaining ten cents of the said thirty cents imposed for the payment of the interest on the present indebtedness of the State, funded in accordance with an Act entitled " an Act to fund the indebtedness of the State" which has accrued or may accrue from April twenty-ninth, eighteen hundred and fifty-one, to December thirty-first, eighteen hundred and fifty-two, (inclusive,) passed May 1st, 1852, and shall constitute the Interest Tax of eighteen hundred and fifty-two, provided in the seventh section of this Act.

Passed April 23rd, 1852.

NOTE.—These are the only Sections of the Revenue Law pertaining to Schools.

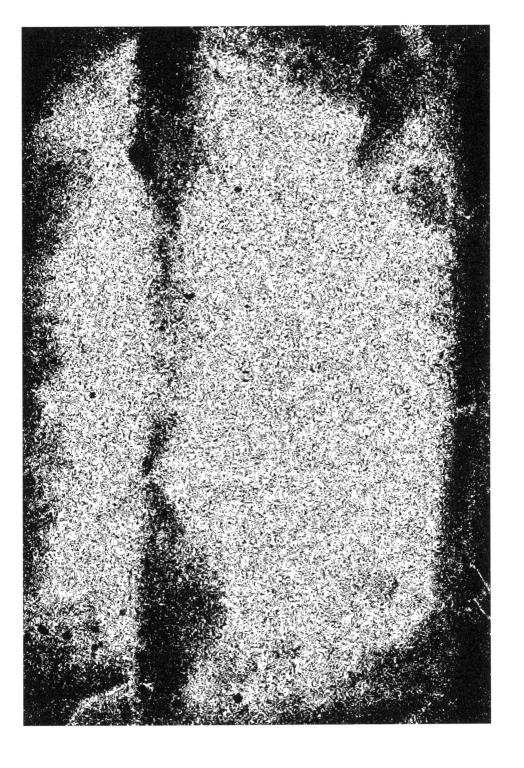

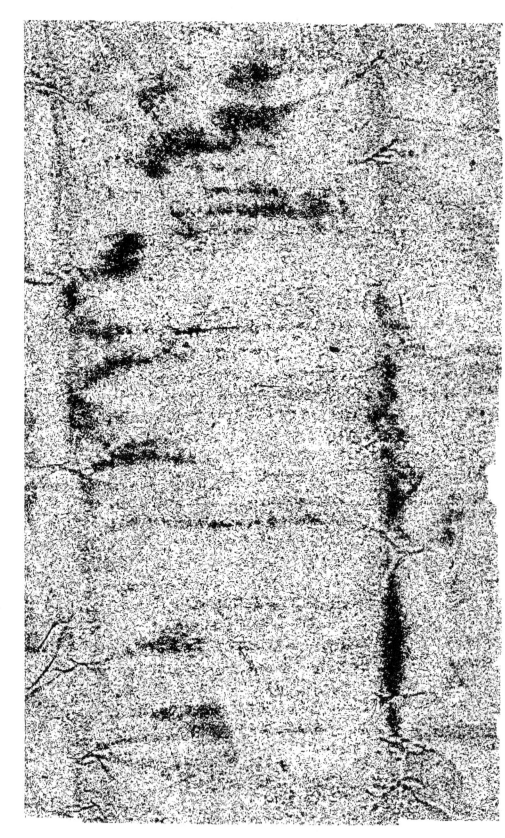

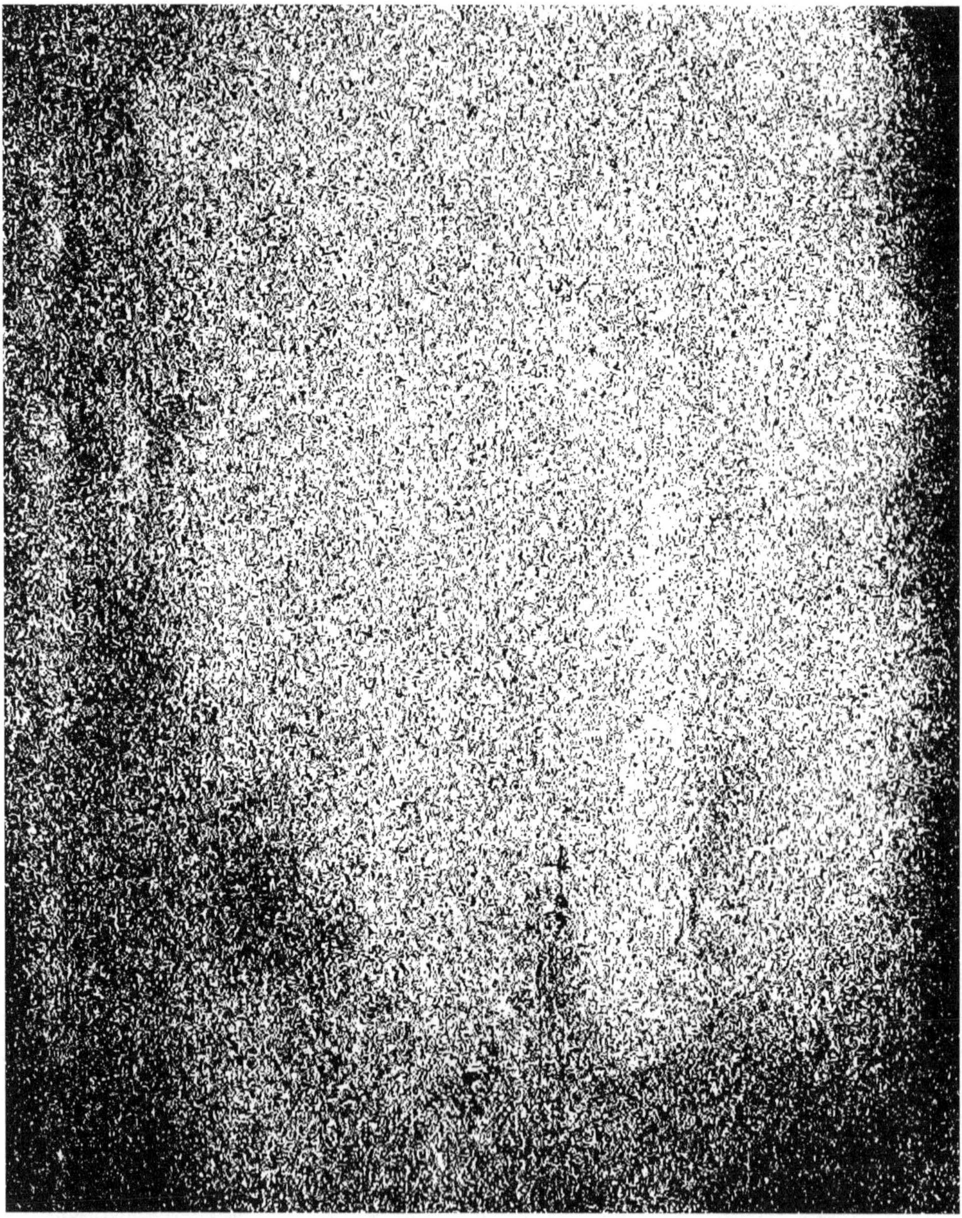

CPSIA information can be obtained
at www.ICGtesting.com
Printed in the USA
BVHW04*1049170918
527708BV00015B/2024/P